For lovers of animals,
history, and especially
raccoons.

Rebecca,
WHITE HOUSE RACCOON

By Kevin Coolidge

Illustrated by Jubal Lee

Everyone loves raccoons. Why, a raccoon could even be president of the United States one day. Did you know that President Calvin Coolidge, America's 30th president, had a pet raccoon?

Her name was Rebecca. She was a gift to President Coolidge. Who wouldn't want a raccoon? A supporter of President Coolidge thought she would be great for Thanksgiving dinner!

Rebecca thought she was invited to Thanksgiving dinner, so was already licking her lips over potatoes and gravy and pumpkin pie, but she was supposed to be the Turkey! People would sometimes eat raccoons. I understand eating rabbits, but raccoons???

The Coolidges did not eat Rebecca. She was too cute to eat. Instead, they adopted her, and even gave her a Christmas present, a collar that read "White House Raccoon."

Rebecca would attend White House events. Her favorite was the annual White House Egg Roll. She would chase the eggs across the White House lawn. She would also play hide and seek. All raccoons are ninjas. She was hard to find!

Rebecca was fed shrimp, persimmons, and eggs. Eggs were her favorite. She was allowed to roam freely in the White House. She would even visit the Oval Office! She would walk on a leash when she went outside.

At times, she was mischievous and was known to unscrew light-bulbs, open cabinets, and unpot houseplants. She also climbed a telephone pole one night and required a firefighter's help to get down.

Raccoons like to keep clean. Rebecca loved playing in the bathtub with a little water in it and would be given a cake of soap to play with. She never forgot to wash behind her ears.

She would go on vacation with the Coolidges. When the president, Calvin, and his wife Grace went to South Dakota, Rebecca went with the dogs—two collies named Rob Roy and Prudence Prim—and five canaries. She even got a postcard of Mount Rushmore.

President Coolidge had many animals over the term of his presidency. Many of them were gifts. The animals included lion cubs, a miniature hippo, and a goose, but the public loved Rebecca most.

The American people loved their presidential raccoon. A man working at the White House decided to find her a boyfriend. He captured a male raccoon, named it Horace, and brought it to the White House to meet Rebecca.

The President did not like the name and changed it to Reuben, but love was not meant to be. Reuben would frequently escape from his cage, to go climb trees and enjoy the outdoors. One time he climbed the fence, and halted traffic on Pennsylvania Avenue for a half hour. He later escaped and was never seen again.

Rebecca would play with White House visitors, and had a special wooden house built just for her. The wooden house had a special panel that she could flip up so she could climb in and out easily.

When the Coolidges left the White House, so did Rebecca. The Coolidges wanted her to live with other raccoons, so they sent Rebecca to the Rock Creek Zoo so she wouldn't be lonely.

Rebbeca the raccoon is now part of American history and the history of the White House. Will raccoons be seen at the White House again? You can count on raccoons to make it happen. Maybe we'll even see a raccoon president one day!

The End

President Calvin Coolidge

Calvin Coolidge served as America's president from 1923 to 1929. He was the only president born on America's birthday July 4th, 1872.

His nickname was "Silent Cal" and many historians refer to him as "the best president you've probably never heard of."

Coolidge married Grace Anna Goodhue, a teacher at a school for the deaf. The couple had two sons, John and Calvin.

Coolidge signed the Indian Citizenship Act, granting full U.S. citizenship to all Native Americans.

He was a man of few words, even until the end. His last will and testament was just 23 words long.

About the Author

Kevin resides in Wellsboro, just a short hike from the Pennsylvania Grand Canyon. When he's not writing, you can find him at From My Shelf Books & Gifts, an independent bookstore he runs with his lovely wife, several helpful employees, and two friendly cats, Huck & Finn.

He's recently become an honorary member of the Cat Board, and when he's not scooping the litter box, or feeding Gypsy her tuna, he's writing more stories about the raccoons, cats, dogs and more. You can find all his books at kevincoolidge.org

You can write him at:

From My Shelf Books & Gifts
7 East Ave
Wellsboro PA 16901
www.wellsborobookstore.com

About the Illustrator

Jubal Lee is a former Wellsboro resident who now resides in sunny Florida, due to his extreme allergic reaction to cold weather. He is an eclectic artist who, when not drawing raccoons, strange creatures, and the like, enjoys writing, bicycling, and short walks on the beach.

Kevin is also the creator of *The Totally Ninja Raccoons*. The books are about three raccoons who decide to become ninjas because they already have the masks. *The Totally Ninja Raccoons* is a series of early chapter books, targeting audiences first through fourth grade.

The books are short adventures with quick chapters, specially structured to encourage reluctant readers. Short chapters, humor, adventure, and one picture per chapter keep kids feeling a sense of engagement and accomplishment as they plow through these stories and ask for more!

Available at *From My Shelf Books & Gifts* on the Internet at www.wellsborobookstore.com, or wherever books are sold.

THE TOTALLY NINJA RACCOONS MEET BIGFOOT

by Kevin Coolidge

THE TOTALLY NINJA RACCOONS MEET THE WEIRD & WACKY WEREWOLF

by Kevin Coolidge

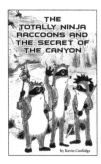

THE TOTALLY NINJA RACCOONS AND THE SECRET OF THE CANYON

by Kevin Coolidge

THE TOTALLY NINJA RACCOONS MEET THE THUNDERBIRD

by Kevin Coolidge

THE TOTALLY NINJA RACCOONS AND THE CATMAS CAPER

THE TOTALLY NINJA RACCOONS AND THE SECRET OF NESSMUK LAKE

by Kevin Coolidge

THE TOTALLY NINJA RACCOONS MEET THE LITTLE GREEN MEN

by Kevin Coolidge

THE TOTALLY NINJA RACCOONS MEET THE JERSEY DEVIL

by Kevin Coolidge

THE TOTALLY NINJA RACCOON JOKE BOOK

by Kevin Coolidge

Kevin's first book, *Hobo Finds A Home*, is a true story about a little kitten. Hobo the Cat leaves the farm, has big adventures, makes a new friend, and finds a forever home.

Hobo was the bookstore cat at *From My Shelf Books & Gifts* for many years. His many jobs included playing with children, delighting cat lovers, and soaking up sunshine to spread to everyone he met. This is his story...

Available at *From My Shelf Books & Gifts*
on the Internet at www.wellsborobookstore.com,
or wherever books are sold.

CPSIA information can be obtained
at www.ICGtesting.com
Printed in the USA
BVHW021134090723
666961BV00005B/34